Create and Share | Thinking Digitally

Using Online Portfolios

By Adrienne Matteson

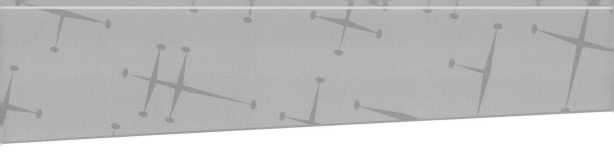

CHERRY LAKE PRESS

Published in the United States of America by Cherry Lake Publishing Group
Ann Arbor, Michigan
www.cherrylakepublishing.com

Series Adviser: Kristin Fontichiaro
Reading Adviser: Marla Conn, MS, Ed., Literacy specialist, Read-Ability, Inc.
Book Designer: Felicia Macheske
Character Illustrator: Rachael McLean

Photo Credits: © Piotr Wawrzyniuk/Shutterstock.com, 5; © wavebreakmedia/Shutterstock.com, 6; © Elizaveta Galitckaia/Shutterstock.com, 9; © Monkey Business Images/Shutterstock.com, 13; © airdone/Shutterstock.com, 15; © Patai Wonganutrohd/Shutterstock.com, 19; © UfaBizPhoto/Shutterstock.com, 21

Graphics Credits Throughout: © the simple surface/Shutterstock.com; © Diana Rich/Shutterstock.com; © lemony/Shutterstock.com; © CojoMoxon/Shutterstock.com; © IreneArt/Shutterstock.com; © Artefficient/Shutterstock.com; © Marie Nimrichterova/Shutterstock.com; © Svetolk/Shutterstock.com; © EV-DA/Shutterstock.com; © briddy/Shutterstock.com; © Mix3r/Shutterstock.com

Cherry Lake Press is an imprint of Cherry Lake Publishing Group.

Library of Congress Cataloging-in-Publication Data has been filed and is available at catalog.loc.gov

Cherry Lake Publishing Group would like to acknowledge the work of the Partnership for 21st Century Learning, a Network of Battelle for Kids. Please visit *http://www.battelleforkids.org/networks/p21* for more information.

Printed in the United States of America
Corporate Graphics

Table of
CONTENTS

CHAPTER ONE

What Is a Portfolio?

Have you ever created something that made you so proud, you wanted to share it with everyone? You make and do amazing things all the time. You do this in school and at home. The things you make and the skills you work hard on are a part of who you are. A great way to remember and share those parts of you is by creating a **digital portfolio**.

Because your portfolio is online, it includes **links** to your creations. This lets you share your **accomplishments** with people who are far away!

What are the things you are most proud of?

How do you share your accomplishments
with your family and friends?

Starting Your Portfolio

Make a list of all of the things you can do that you are really proud of. They can be anything. But try to focus on skills you worked hard on. Do you like to write books or draw? What about make putty or dance? You can add almost anything to your digital portfolio. Are you proud of what you built in *Minecraft*? What about the computer program you coded in Scratch 3.0? List all of the things that show off your skills and personality. This list is the beginning of your portfolio.

CHAPTER TWO

Getting Started

Before creating your portfolio, you need to decide what site to use. Sometimes it costs money to create a website. Other companies will give you the tools to make a simple website and then **host** it for free. These sites include Weebly, WordPress, and Google Sites. Seesaw is another popular **platform** that many students use to create their digital portfolio. Aside from Seesaw, most portfolio-creation services require the user to be at least 13 years old. Because of this, always ask a trusted adult for help. Adults can assist with creating an online account and setting a safe password. They can also help you narrow down what your digital portfolio should look like.

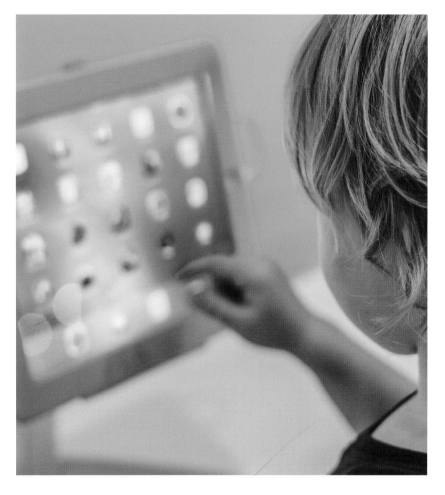

Create a home page that tells everyone who you are with words and pictures.

Once you have decided where to host your website, it's time to create it! A website usually has a home page and many other pages that link back to the home page. Begin with a home page that tells who you are and what visitors can expect to find in your portfolio.

Be careful about what you include when you describe yourself and your portfolio. You don't want to put any information on the internet that identifies you, your location, or your school.

Do you know how to make a website? If not, Weebly and Google Sites are easy to learn. Before you know it, you'll have a website that will reflect your personality!

Plan It Out

It's always best to have a plan. Try sketching out what you want your online portfolio to look like. Be sure to include the home page and the pages for your different skills and projects. Also, think about what you want to include in your portfolio. Portfolios aren't meant to include everything you've ever done. Instead, they should reflect your best work and the work that shows how much you've improved.

Do Include:

- Who you are and what you like (Examples: "I love making movies and playing soccer" or "I like drawing and coding")
- Special projects you have been working on
- Skills you are working hard to learn, like knitting or coding

Do Not Include:

- Your last name
- Your address or phone number
- The name of your school

Never share your full name, school, or address online.
Your safety is important.

CHAPTER THREE

What Goes in a Portfolio?

It's time to show off! Your portfolio should be full of things you have done or made that make you proud. Now that you have a home page, you can add pages with the skills and projects you want to share with others. You should group similar things together so each page has a main subject.

Do you have schoolwork that you want to share, such as writing or art? Scan or take a photo of it, and **upload** the image to your website. Remember to cover or crop out personal information, like your name and the name of your school. Be sure to include a **description** of what the assignment was. And don't forget to add a quick note about why you've included it in your portfolio.

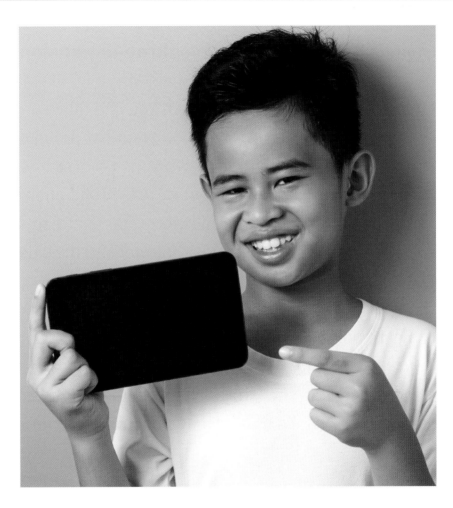

Take pictures and videos of projects that are not digital.

Do you want to share projects that are **three-dimensional** (3D), like a LEGO creation? Is your project very big, like a fort or a treehouse? If so, then make a video. You can move around and describe what it is and the parts you are most proud of.

Do you have an Hour of Code project or a YouTube channel you want to include? It's easy to add work that is already on the internet to your new portfolio. Visit the website the video or project is on. Copy the **URL** and use it to create a link on a page in your portfolio. If you have trouble finding the URL, look for the word Share on the original website.

You can add new pages anytime you have more work to share. Just like you, your portfolio will grow and change over time.

Organizing Your Portfolio

Look back at your list from chapter 1. Can you group your skills into categories, such as writing, art, inventions, or sports? On a piece of paper or a whiteboard, divide the things you want to include in your portfolio into similar groups. Write down anything you might need to take pictures and videos of. Note any URLs you need to get. Also, make a note of anything you did with a partner or group. Be sure to ask permission and give credit to your partners when you put their work online. But do this before creating your website! It's easier to have a clear idea of how you want to organize your portfolio before you design your website.

Always give credit online to your partners when you post work they helped with.

CHAPTER FOUR

Growing Together

Your portfolio is something you are making for your future self. You will be able to look at it and see all of the skills you have learned and how much you have improved. That means you should return to your portfolio to add new things and make changes.

You should post new skills or projects as soon as you have done them. As you improve, continue to add more to that page. You'll be able to see how far you have come.

In your portfolio, include activities you are just starting.
That way, you can show how much you improve.

You might also want to include a **blog** or **vlog** section in your portfolio. You can use this to describe new things you are working on and accomplishments you are excited about.

Remember to **update** the description on your home page at least once a year. You may decide to change other things as you get older. The design and **layout**, the pictures on your home page, and even the projects you share might all change. For instance, you might think about removing older work as you add new work to your portfolio.

Share Your Portfolio

There are many ways you can share your digital portfolio. You can tell your friends during recess or your family during get-togethers. You can also share it online. If you have a blog, write a post describing why you decided to make a portfolio. Are you or an adult you trust on social media? With a parent's permission, you can share your portfolio on Instagram, Facebook, Twitter, YouTube, or even TikTok! Discuss the ways you can share your portfolio on these different social platforms.

Your portfolio should keep changing and growing just like you!

GLOSSARY

accomplishments (uh-KAHM-plish-muhnts) things you have succeeded at doing or making

blog (BLAWG) a website that acts like an online journal

description (dih-SKRIP-shuhn) a written or spoken statement that tells about someone or something

digital portfolio (DIJ-ih-tuhl port-FOH-lee-oh) an online collection of pictures, videos, and links that shows off what you are most proud of

host (HOHST) a computer that stores all the pages of a website and makes them available to computers connected to the internet

layout (LAY-out) where everything is placed on a web page

links (LINGKS) pieces of text on a web page that connect to another web page when clicked

platform (PLAT-form) the online service you use to create a website

three-dimensional (THREE duh-MEN-shuhn-uhl) not flat, commonly written as 3D

update (UHP-date) to provide the latest information

upload (UHP-lohd) to send information to another computer over a network

URL (YOO AR EL) stands for uniform resource locator; it is the "address" you type into a browser to find a web page

vlog (VLAWG) a video blog in which the entries are videos instead of writings

BOOKS

Fontichiaro, Kristin. *Building a Blog*. Ann Arbor, MI: Cherry Lake Publishing, 2020.

Hatter, Clyde. *Create with Code: Build Your Own Website*. New York, NY: Scholastic/CoderDojo Foundation, 2017.

WEBSITES

Artsonia
https://www.artsonia.com
Check out the largest online collection of student art.

Seesaw
https://web.seesaw.me
Easily create and share your online portfolio using Seesaw.

INDEX

About the AUTHOR

Adrienne Matteson is a middle school librarian in Atlanta, Georgia. When she is not teaching her students to be good digital citizens, she is knitting, singing, and serving the community.